The Key Stage 1 **Poetry pack**

Alan Peat

QUESTIONS
PUBLISHING

The *Questions* Publishing Company Limited
Birmingham
2003

First Published in 2003 by
The *Questions* Publishing Company Ltd
321 Bradford Street, Birmingham B5 6ET

Edited by: Amanda Greenley
Design: Al Stewart and James Davies
Illustrations: Iqbal Aslam

ISBN: 1-84190-100-8

Also available from *Questions* Publishing Company:
The Key Stage 2 Poetry Pack
ISBN: 1-84190-044-3

Acknowledgements

My sincere thanks to my father for his continued help and encouragement and to Sally for the same. This book would not have been possible without long holidays in hot places.

"If I were a medical man, I should prescribe a holiday to any patient who considered his work important." Bertrand Russell

'Dis/continuities' by Andrew Taylor, from *Götterdämmerung Cafè*, (University of Queensland Press, 2001) is reproduced by permission of University of Queensland Press.

'A Who'Z Who of the Horrible House' by Wes Magee, from *The Works,* chosen by Paul Cookson (MacMillan Children's Books, 2000) is reproduced by permission of MacMillan Children's Books.

Dedication

For Niesha and Kasai Rimmer with lots of love from Uncle Alan.

Contents

Introduction

Throughout the Foundation Stage and Key Stage 1, it is absolutely imperative that we nurture in pupils a 'love of language' and model this for them. Poetry is an ideal vehicle for such nurturing as its structured playfulness can be mimicked and developed in pupils' own work.

The Key Stage 1 Poetry Pack has been written with the enjoyment of poetry as its prime purpose. It has also been written with busy classroom practitioners in mind and, as such, each poem is explicitly linked to a National Literacy Framework objective. As with the companion volume, *The Key Stage 2 Poetry Pack,* a 'Teachers' Notes' section accompanies each poem. Suggestions for activities and extension ideas are detailed on the page adjacent to the poem/s.

Reading and enjoying poetry undoubtedly has a positive impact on pupils' poetry writing. Consequently, the breadth of poetry forms they experience is of fundamental importance. The range should include:

- poems with repeating patterns,
- action poems and counting rhymes,
- poems from a range of different cultures,
- poems written by the children themselves (both displayed around the classroom and in book format on the library shelves),
- rhyming and non-rhyming poems,
- themed collections,
- collections by individual poets, and
- published poems with pupils' responses (e.g. transformations/ extensions) collected as class anthologies*.

The poems chosen for this collection have been used in 'Book Week' and 'Author Workshop' contexts with pupils in infant classrooms around the UK – and have all passed the stringent 'pupil-response' test! As enjoyment should be of paramount importance when using the material included in this book, worksheet-driven approaches are best avoided.

How to use this book

In order to ensure ease of use, this collection is in line with the National Literacy Framework's year and term objectives. It begins with poems that can be used to facilitate the Reception text level objectives for reading and writing poetry, and concludes with poems linked to the Year 2 Term 3 objectives.

A range of rhyming and non-rhyming (free verse) poems has been included in this volume. When augmenting these poems with personal favourites, it is hoped that teachers will also select rhyming and non-rhyming examples so that pupils do not come to regard rhyming poems as the norm.

*This list can be used by literacy co-ordinators and class teachers in order to audit the variety of poetry forms available to pupils in the classroom.

The framework objectives referred to throughout the book are described by year then term followed by 'T' (Text level) and the number of the objective as specified in the framework, e.g. Year 1, Term 2, T.13.

Language games and poetry

Any activity that encourages pupils to play with language will have a beneficial impact in terms of literacy development. A number of these 'language games' are discussed in the 'Teachers' Notes' sections throughout this book. It should be stressed that such games are not just for playing when a specific Literacy Strategy objective needs to be met – such a narrow usage would certainly limit their impact. Instead teachers should aim to use language games whenever possible as they:

- are beneficial (in 'short burst' form) as a refocusing mechanism,
- make ideal motivational lesson openers,
- can often be used in a cross-curricular context, and
- assist in developing an enjoyment of language.

Purists may challenge whether the end results of some of the activities included here are actually 'poems' in the strictest sense. In the context of an adult poetry collection this would be justified, but if one recognises that the primary purpose of this book is to excite and interest pupils in both reading and writing poetry, then I trust readers will agree that the activities more than achieve this aim.

The Key Stage 1 Poetry Pack
Poems and Teachers' Notes

KS1 poem

Where?

Where is the pencil, where can it be?
Let's look around until we see.

It's
on the desk,
above the floor,
under the ceiling,
near the door,
left of the watertray,
right of the sand,
I've picked it up
It's in my hand!

Where is the pencil, where can it be?
Let's look around until we see.

Where?

Where? is a poem that is ideally suited to actions, thereby encouraging participation and lending an enjoyable multi-sensory element to group/class recitation.

Activity one: Group/class recitation with actions

When using the poem for this purpose, model actions: begin with your hand above your eyes (as if searching), to focus on the first word – 'where'. This is followed by a series of actions specifically linked to the range of prepositions used in the poem.

Preposition	Action
on	pat the floor OR smooth hand across floor
above	point to the ceiling/sky
under	put hand under a desk or left hand under right (if sat on the carpet!)
near	two hands close together, but not touching
left	point to the left (remember that this will be to *your* right if you are demonstrating!)
right	point to the right (remember that this will be to *your* left if you are demonstrating!)

The use of actions helps to enhance pupils' understanding of the meaning of each preposition. Once modelled, the children can 'join in' and/or suggest their own actions for other words in the poem.

Activity two: Change the subject

If you wish to encourage pupils to experiment with the pattern of the poem, this can easily be achieved by choosing a different object in the classroom. The opening of each line will remain the same, but the endings will depend upon where the object is in the classroom. For example, if you choose a clock it could be:

on the wall,
above the desk,
under the poster,
near the window, etc.

If pupils take it in turns to play this game, then their answers can be used to determine their understanding and application of the prepositions used in the poem.

National Literacy Strategy Links

Reception T.10: to re-read and recite stories and rhymes with predictable and repeated patterns and experiment with similar rhyming patterns.

KS1 poem

I'm not! I never! I don't! I can't!

I'm not as HUGE as a whale in the sea
I'm not as small as a busy, buzzing bee,
I cannot skip or jump or hop
I cannot whistle, click or pop,
I do not speak, I cannot fly
I don't tell truth, I never lie
And I don't even comb my hair
I have no mirror, I don't care
But sometimes when no-one's around
I leap about and make these sounds
SPLOSH! and SPLASH! and also SPLISH!
You've guessed, my friend, I am a fish.

I'm not! I never! I don't! I can't!

This poem consists of a series of negatives. As a result, the predictable, repetitive nature of the structure lends itself well to both oral composition and extension work.

Activity one: What isn't it?

Read the poem on the opposite page to the pupils (as a modelled example). Then ask them to choose a different animal or object. The oral scaffold heightens the cognitive demand of the activity. The following example has proved reliable in workshops conducted with a broad range of Reception aged pupils:

> I'm not...
> I'm not...
> I don't...
> I don't...
> I have no...
> I have no...
> I cannot...
> I cannot...
> I am a/an...*

Write down pupils' oral suggestions for the conclusion to each line. This ensures that opportunities for modelling the writing process can be maximised later.

Activity two: The fish goes splish!

To begin this activity, repeat your 'favourite' line: *SPLOSH! and SPLASH! and also SPLISH!* A list poem is then produced beginning with this line. Pupils can then suggest other lines. If they find this difficult you can provide line openers as you did in Activity one. Some suggestions are:

> The drum goes...
> The lion goes...
> The mouse goes...
> The clock goes...

Children may imitate a sound rather than using the correct onomatopoeic word, e.g. making a roaring sound instead of saying 'roar'. If this occurs, then a game of 'turning sounds into words' (with you making the sounds) can help.

A variation of this activity is writing 'Noisy sounds' poems and 'Quiet sounds' poems. Choose sentence starters for each poem in order to ensure that pupils produce an appropriate list poem.

N.B. The opportunity to discuss why the word 'HUGE' is produced in a larger font size and the word 'small' is produced in a smaller font size should not be missed. An early grasp of typographical conventions, such as these, can produce a useful 'hook' for stimulating pupils' interest in language.

National Literacy Strategy Links

Year 1 Term 1 T.6: to recite stories and rhymes with predictable and repeating patterns, extemporising on patterns orally by substituting words and phrases, extending patterns, inventing patterns and playing with rhyme.

Teachers' notes

5

*Consider substituting other sentence openers to make useful links to the High Frequency Word List in the National Literacy Strategy Framework.

A, B, C and Tumble Down D

A, B, C and tumble down D,
The cat's in the cupboard and can't see me

E, F, G, H, I, J, K,
I think he might have run away

L, M, N, O, P, Q, R,
He's come right back so he didn't go far

S, T, U, V, W, X, Y,
If I lost him I would cry

And now we come, at last, to Z,
He's sleeping safely on my bed.

KS1 poem

A, B, C and Tumble Down D

This variation on a traditional poem reinforces pupils' understanding of alphabetical order in a fun way. It also provides opportunities for substituting alternative words and phrases.

Activity one: Change–a–line

The purpose of this activity is to encourage pupils to suggest alternatives to the second, fourth, sixth and eighth lines (thereby playing with rhyme). If the concept of substituting words is not fully understood, then a preliminary activity that works well is 'Either/or'. To play this, read aloud an alphabet line, e.g.

A, B, C, and tumble down <u>*D,*</u>

ensuring that the final rhyming letter is accentuated. Ask the pupils to choose a word that rhymes with that letter and give them two alternatives – 'either/or'. Some suggestions are:

D – knee/hand   R – bus/car
K – dance/play   Y – fly/drive

The 'Change–a–line' activity can then be played using the chosen rhyming words:

A, B, C, and tumble down D,
I've just landed on my knee

Activity two: Find a letter

Beginning*	Aa	...etc...	Zz	End

To play this, provide each pupil with an alphabet strip.

Point to a letter (on an enlarged copy of the poem) and ask the pupils to find and point to the same letter on their alphabet strip. Ask if the letter is near the 'Beginning' or the 'End' of the strip. If the children cope well with this then they can use a dictionary instead of the alphabet strip. For example,

Teacher: Can you find the letter 'D' on your strip?
Pupil: There! (Pointing to Dd)
Teacher: Very good. Is that near the beginning of the alphabet (pointing
    to the word 'Beginning' on the alphabet strip) or near the end (again
    pointing) to the strip?
Pupil: Beginning.
Teacher: Excellent. So do you think the letter 'D' will be near the
    beginning or the end of the dictionary?
Pupil: Beginning.
Teacher: Now open the dictionary at the beginning and see if you can find
    that letter.

This activity helps pupils understand how to access words in a dictionary and reinforces their knowledge of alphabetical order.

*The word 'start' can be substituted for 'Beginning' if prefered.

National Literacy Strategy Links

Year 1 Term 1 T.6: to recite stories and rhymes with predictable and repeating patterns, extemporising on patterns orally by substituting words and phrases, extending patterns, inventing patterns and playing with rhyme.

KS1 poem

1, 2, 3, 4, 5

1, 2, 3, 4, 5
Once I caught a fish alive

6, 7, 8, 9, 10
After that I caught a hen

11, 12 and 13 too
If this goes on I'll start a zoo!

1, 2, 3, 4, 5

There is a tradition of using counting rhymes with young children as a means of reinforcing their understanding of ordinal numbers. The example given is a variation of one such rhyme and can easily be used as a model for the pupils' own writing. The following strategies can assist pupils.

Activity one: A 'Things I do' poem

Pupils can write a 'Things I do' poem, based on the poem opposite, by changing each of the even lines, the non-numerical lines, into lines about things they do. If they find this difficult begin by reading aloud the poem below, pausing at the words in bold to see if the pupils can say each one before it is read out. This usually proves an adequate starting point for their own version.

> *1, 2, 3, 4, 5*
> *At the baths I like to **dive***
>
> *6, 7, 8, 9, 10*
> *When I write I use a **pen***
>
> *11, 12 and 13 too*
> *These are things I like to **do***

Activity two: An 'Even numbers' poem

An 'Even numbers' poem is written by breaking each line after an even number:

> *One, two*
> *Unbuckle my shoe*
>
> *Three, four*
> *Open the door*

The resulting poem does **not** have to make sense, as the objective is to create rhyming patterns.

As an extension activity, more able pupils can be asked to extend the original poem using:

> *14, 15, 16 next...*
>
> *17, 18 after that...*
>
> *19, 20 which comes last!*

National Literacy Strategy Links

Year 1 Term 1 T.10: to use rhymes and patterned stories as models for their own writing.

KS1 *poem*

ME!

I've got ten fingers – great to count!
I've got a mouth and it can shout,
I've got two legs and they can run,
I've got one smile when life is fun,
I've got two eyes to help me see,
And that's about the whole of me.

ME!

Action poems provide an excellent medium for engaging pupils in 'language-play'; they also appeal to kinaesthetic learners and should form a significant part of all poetry teaching in the early years.

A useful preliminary activity when using the poem *ME!* is to ask the pupils to invent their own actions. This leads to active engagement with the poem and creates a sense of 'ownership' among the pupils.

The following activities can produce new 'action poems'.

Activity one: More of me

This poem is basically an extension of the one opposite. Encourage pupils to suggest other parts of the body that can be added to the opening *I've got....* For example, *I've got one nose...*

Following this a 'sentence modifier' is needed – either *and it can...* or *and they can....* An example of a finished line may read:

> *I've got one nose and it can sniff*

Do not be concerned about creating a rhyming poem but aim to help pupils create a patterned series of lines with appropriate actions.

Activity two: Around our class

This simple activity is based on the same principle as *ME!* but rather than creating lines which (i) identify parts of the body and (ii) explain their function, pupils produce lines which (i) identify objects around the classroom and (ii) explain their function. For example,

> *We've got two fish and they can swim*

The outcome of each of these activities, is a list poem with identical line openings: a useful mechanism for learning words in the High Frequency Word List!

National Literacy Strategy Links

Year 1 Term 2 T.11: to learn and recite simple poems and rhymes, with actions, and to re-read them from the text.

A Who'Z Who of the Horrible House

Wes Magee

Inside
the
Horrible
House
there is
an awful aquamarine apparition abseiling
a bug-eyed beige bogeyman boxing
a cackling crimson cockroach creeping
a disgusting damson Dracula dancing
an eerie emerald elf electrocuting
a floppy flame Frankenstein fencing
a grotty green ghost groaning
a haunting hazel hag hammering
an insane indigo imp ice-screaming
a jittery jade jackal juggling
a kinky khaki king knitting
a loony lime leprechaun lassooing
a monocled maroon madman marching
a nightmarish navy nastie nipping
an outrageous orange ogre oozing
a phoolish purple phantom phoning
a quadruple quicksilver quagga quaking
a revolting red rattlesnake rock 'n' rolling
a spotty scarlet spectre spitting
a terrible turquoise troll trampolining
an ugly umber uncle umpiring
a violent violet vampire vibrating
a whiskery white werewolf windsurfing
an eXcitable xanthic eXoskeleton eXploding
a yucky yellow yak yelling
a zitty zinc zombie zapping
inside
the
Horrible
House!

KS1 poem

A Who'Z Who of the Horrible House
(Wes Magee)

The alliterative, alphabetical structure of this poem never fails to captivate pupils. It provides an excellent starting point for the development of pupils' own alliterative poems due to its tightly controlled structure, which is easy to replicate.

After reading the poem, ask pupils to name as many animals as possible. Write these suggestions on a large sheet of paper, or on the board, alongside their corresponding letter of the alphabet. Ask careful questions to encourage the children to think of an alliterative adjective to place before the named animal. For example, if a pupil suggested a 'bat' then you could ask for a word that means the opposite of 'small': *A big bat.*

Use a similar questioning technique to produce an alliterative verb to place after the named animal. You could also dramatise what the animal might be doing, e.g. blowing the pages of a book: *A big bat blowing.*

You can continue with this process of shared writing until you have produced a complete poem, or you may wish to only model three or four lines before asking groups of pupils to complete the poem.

National Literacy Strategy Links

Year 1 Term 2 T.13: to substitute and extend patterns from reading through language play, e.g. by using same lines and introducing new words, extending rhyming or alliterative patterns, adding further rhyming words, lines.

Family Poems

My gran's got a motorbike

Come sun or hail or rain or snow
My gran's dressed, she's got to go!
Whatever form or type of weather
On goes gran's protective leather

She doesn't drive or sail or hike
My gran's got a motorbike!

She likes to ride and see the view
From her B.M.W.,
But watch her and you'll see she's fonder
of her nicely polished Honda

She doesn't drive or sail or hike
My gran's got a motorbike!

The first one she was ever caught on
Was her dad's expensive Norton,
Its chrome would shine, its wheels would gleam,
She even liked the headlight beam!

She doesn't drive or sail or hike
My gran's got a motorbike!

But on her Harley Davidson
I'm sad to say she did 'the ton',
Her teeth shot out – it didn't suit her,
So now she only rides a scooter.

She still won't drive or sail or hike
At night she dreams of motorbikes.

My Baby Brother

It was ace…having a baby brother!
it meant I was never last
in running, hopping, jumping races
it meant I always won
the 'Who is tallest?' competition
it meant I was never a baddie…
…he was!
When my friends and I played 'Scientists'
and we made our special
brown sauce, milk, salt and lemonade potion
there was always someone to try it!
It was ace…having a baby brother,
Even if he sometimes got angry
For no reason at all!

KS1 poem

15

Dad's into D.I.Y.

KS1 poem

Dad's into D.I.Y.
Shelves are leaning…ask us why?
Dad's into D.I.Y.

The roof's collapsing,
Taps are leaking
Mum and Dad are hardly speaking
Why such trouble?…this is why
Dad's into D.I.Y.

The washer leaves a flooded floor,
Rooms now have lost their doors,
The fish tank's dry and the fish are in it
If we see Dad's hammer we just bin it,
It's a problem, why oh why
Is dad into D.I.Y.?

Around our house a paint smell lingers,
He hammers nails into his fingers,
Trips on tools, spills carpet cleaner
On the dog, who's getting meaner,
All because…and you know why…
My dad's into D.I.Y.!

Family Poems

The two main advantages of reading themed groups of poems with pupils are that they:

- offer opportunities for combining literacy with other areas of the curriculum. When linking poetry to other work being undertaken in class, it will be regarded as a part of the whole rather than as a marginalised/isolated aspect of learning.
- allow pupils to compare and contrast, which can be used to develop an understanding of the structural basis of many poems.

The three poems included here were chosen for their structural variety. *My gran's got a motorbike* rhymes in couplets and has a repeating chorus. *My Baby Brother* is an example of free verse (no rhyming structure). *Dad's into D.I.Y.* has a more fluid rhyming pattern that includes both **triplets**:

> *The roofs collapsing*
> *Taps are leaking*
> *Mum and Dad are hardly speaking*

and **couplets**:

> *Around our house a paint smell lingers*
> *He hammers nails into his fingers.*

A discussion of the similarities and differences between these three poems can be used as an introduction to the activities below:

Activity one
Collect pupils' favourite poems on a theme and make a book entitled *Our Class Book of Favourite Poems about....*

Activity two
Write a range of different kinds of poems (such as the forms discussed in this book) in order to produce a book entitled *Our Class Book of Favourite Poems about....* The publication of pupils' poems in book format, and the inclusion of this in a class (or school) library, is a useful means of motivating pupils and helping them to view themselves as authors.

It may be useful for you to consider varying the format of a class anthology by shaping the pages of the book appropriately, i.e. having pages shaped like flowers for a class anthology of poems on the subject of 'plants'.

National Literacy Strategy Links

Year 1 Term 3 T.9: to read a variety of poems on similar themes, e.g. families, school, food.

Teachers' notes

Reading Aloud Together!
How can we make it better?

Have we thought about…

…saying some parts loudly and some parts quietly?

…saying some parts quickly and some parts slowly?

…reading some of the lines together?

…choosing individuals (or small groups) to say some of the lines by themselves?

…not standing still? Try moving your arms or legs. If the poem has a word like 'wave' in it you could 'wave' your hands. Are there any words in your poem that could have actions?

…using our faces? If the poem has a word like 'scared' you could look scared! Are there any words in your poem that you could make faces for?

…speaking so everyone can hear?

Don't forget to look at your audience.

Good luck!

Reading Aloud Together!

Reading aloud

Reading poems aloud can either be a useful and enjoyable aspect of poetry teaching or a meaningless 'time-filler'. To avoid the latter, we need to consider how to help pupils become more confident and more effective at reading aloud.

In order to develop pupils' confidence it is necessary for you to model reading poems aloud. Likewise, you can model a range of strategies to help children make their own reading aloud more effective. These include:

- changes in volume and intonation,
- changes in tempo,
- methods of dramatising the poems – through, for example, use of appropriate actions and/or facial expressions, and
- talking to the audience rather than to the poem!

These strategies can be discussed explicitly with the pupils. The photocopiable poster opposite can be used to draw attention to particular techniques. You can use the sheet as:

- a stimulus for improving whole-class reading,
- a 'reminder' for smaller groups preparing to read a chosen poem aloud.

Whole-class reading should precede small group reading. Gradually handing over the responsibility for effective reading of a poem will help to develop pupils' confidence and enjoyment of poetry.

National Literacy Strategy Links

Year 1 Term 3 T.11: to collect class and individual favourite poems for class anthologies, participate in reading aloud.

Phew! What a week

On Monday we
            moved house and
            mowed the lawn.
On Tuesday we
            threw boxes in the bin and
            took a trip to the tip.
On Wednesday we
            weeded the garden and
            walked the dog.
On Thursday we
            tidied the living room and
            tarmaced the drive.
On Friday we
            fixed the fence and
            framed some pictures.
On Saturday we
            stacked shelves and
            swept the carpets.
On Sunday we
            sighed with relief and
            slept like babies.
Phew! What a week!

Phew! What a week

Phew! What a week is ideally suited for discussing and developing poems with related structures. This 'transformational approach' can be applied to any of the poems in this book, and helps pupils to understand how to organise words into poems.

Activity one: Phew! What a year

Introduce this activity (after reading *Phew! What a week*) by telling the pupils that they are about to write a poem about the 'hardest year ever'. On the board, write *In January we...* (note the underlined '*J*'). Ask pupils to name the months of the year, in sequence, until you reach *In December we....* Pupils can then provide examples of difficult things they could do. You may need to use careful questioning to encourage answers that use alliteration and are seasonally appropriate. For example,

> *In December we dug the snow*

Alternatively, use the same approach, but with Seasons instead of months. For example,

> *In Spring we...*
> *In Summer we...*

Activity two: The laziest week ever!

You may find that this activity works best if alliteration is avoided. A useful approach is to concentrate on opposites. Give pupils a line from 'the busiest week ever' and ask them to provide an appropriate opposite.

Busiest	Laziest
On Monday I ran about.	On Monday I lay down all day.
On Tuesday I talked for hours.	On Tuesday I didn't speak, I only yawned...

Activity three: The week we travelled all over!

Give pupils the sentence starters:

> *On Monday we went to...*
> *On Tuesday we went to...*

Ask them to suggest geographical locations, using alliteration (a map or atlas may be used and you can specify either countries or places in the UK). The finished poem could read:

> *On Monday we went to Manchester*
> *On Tuesday we went to Twickenham*
> *On Wednesday we went to Wimbledon...*

National Literacy Strategy Links

Year 1 Term 3 T.15: to use poems or parts of poems as models for own writing, e.g. by substituting words or elaborating on the text.

Teachers' notes

What to be today?

Some days I'm…
            sad as a swimming pool drowned beetle,
            still as a headlight-caught cat,
            slow as a river cutting corners from the earth.
Other days I'm…
            glad as a Christmas morning wake up,
            mobile as a feather riding the breeze,
            fast as a coin in a pocket to a sweet shop.
Today…

            so far, I haven't made my mind up.

KS1 poem

What to be today?

What to be today? is a type of list poem. The repetitive pattern is formed of 'simile sentences' – a simple type of poetic sentence that can be developed with older Year 1 pupils.

First, develop pupils' understanding of simile, through the use of 'Feely Boxes'. (A 'Feely Box' contains objects which the children can touch – usually through a hole in the side – but cannot see.)

Produce two 'Feely Boxes', one of which contains *only rough* objects whilst the other contains *only smooth* objects. Also select one rough object, such as a piece of bark, and one smooth object, such as a pebble. Keep these out of the boxes.

Write two sentence starters on the board, with the two objects that are not in the boxes as their subjects.

> *The pebble is as smooth as…*
> *The bark is as rough as…*

Invite individual pupils to feel inside the appropriate box and, by touch alone, guess what an object is *before* they take it out. They then complete the sentence. If sandpaper is taken from the box of rough objects, the sentence becomes: *The bark is as rough as sandpaper*. Repeat this until the children have produced a range of simile sentences. Explain that a simile compares one thing with another. The tactile nature of this exercise helps pupils to retain an understanding of what a simile is in their long-term memory.

Having written a 'Feely Box' poem, the children can work on a 'Simile opposites' poem. This is comprised of alternating lines of opposites. For example,

> *Today it was as hot as…*
> *Yesterday it was as cold as…*
> *Today it was as hot as…*
> *Yesterday it was as cold as…*

Other suggestions for 'Simile opposites' poems are:

> *The road was as bendy as…*
> *The other road was as straight as…*

> *The snail was as slow as…*
> *The hare was as fast as…*

If the children find 'simile sentences' hard to understand, then alliterative sentences will also facilitate Year 1 Term 3 T.16. The poem *A Who'Z Who of the Horrible House* by Wes Magee (reproduced on page 12) provides a useful starting point for work on alliterative sentences.

National Literacy Strategy Links

Year 1 Term 3 T.16: to compose own poetic sentences, using repetitive patterns, carefully selected sentences and imagery.

The Worm's Tale

KS1 poem

I have no ears, I have no eyes,
I like things wet, but I hate things dry,
See me burrow and see me squirm,
I'm a twisting, turning, wiggling worm,
And there's something I've done since birth,
Chomped and chewed my way through earth,
I'm not bad, there are beasts much meaner,
But I am Nature's vacuum cleaner,
You know I'm wiggling through the ground,
But you can't hear me make a sound,
See me as I work and toil,
Taking care of your garden's soil!

CHOMP!
CHEW!

The Worm's Tale

The Worm's Tale is an example of a poem that integrates presentation and subject matter: one of the most effective variations on the standard layout of a poem.

In *The Worm's Tale* the lines 'wiggle like worms'. After looking at and reading the poem, ask pupils why they think the lines aren't straight. Once you have established that they mimic the worm's movement, ask pupils to suggest other ideas for poems that could 'look different on the page'. Suggestions for successful poems are:

- The sun/summer (lines radiating around an inner circle)

- The sea/seaside (waves)

- Castles (turrets)

- Mountains (peaks)

This approach can then be developed into 'concrete poems' (often referred to as 'shape poems') – poems that set in the shape of the subject. You can produce a stencil for the pupils, which they draw around and write inside.

Football stencil

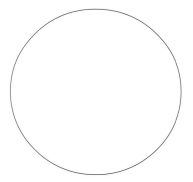

Completed example

I love to
play football
I run in the park
I kick it for hours
It makes me really happy
It's better than T.V.
It keeps me
fit

You can also model changing the size of handwriting in a poem. For example,

Large font – ELEPHANT
Small font – mouse
Large font – NOISY
Small font – quiet

National Literacy Strategy Links

Year 2 Term 1 T.7: to learn, re-read and recite favourite poems... to comment on aspects such as word combinations, sound patterns (such as rhymes, rhythms, alliterative patterns) and forms of presentation.

Teachers' notes

There's a Monkey in my House!

It's distressing! It's upsetting! Shouldn't happen in your home,
There's a monkey in my house and it won't leave me alone!

It was bouncing in the bedrooms and the bed legs all went
   CRUNCH!
It fed the dog a turkey that was meant to be my lunch,
It ran a bath then ran off and the water all ran over
I can't say that I like it but it's popular with Rover.

It's distressing! It's upsetting! Shouldn't happen in your home,
There's a monkey in my house and it won't leave me alone!

It hurls cushions in the living room, does cartwheels in the
   hall,
Wreaks havoc with the flower beds when it's out playing ball,
Bangs biscuit tins with wooden spoons, hurls mud at drying
   sheets,
Leaves slippery banana skins right beneath my feet.

It's distressing! It's upsetting! Shouldn't happen in your home,
There's a monkey in my house and it won't leave me alone!

It turns the Hi-Fi volume up until the house walls shake,
Things vibrate, then fall off shelves and very often break,
It thinks there's treasure in the garden – digs up all the flowers!
It's worryingly silent then it wails for hours and hours!

It's distressing! It's upsetting! Shouldn't happen in your home,
There's a monkey in my house and it won't leave me alone!

My hair's turned grey since he arrived, I fear things could
   get worse
But I cannot bear to go on so I'm going to end this verse,
There's a monkey in my house and believe me it's no fun,
I'd throw him out this instant but he tells me he's my son!!

There's a Monkey in my House!

There's a Monkey in my House! was written particularly for recital – it is constructed from rhyming couplets with a repeating chorus. Many words in the poem lend themselves to actions and an alliterative third line has been included. In order to help pupils develop their poetry recital skills, remember to use the photocopiable sheet 'Reading Aloud Together! How can we make it better?' (on page 18).

Using questions to develop closer scrutiny of a poem

A useful activity for refining pupils' understanding of the organisation/structure of a poem is through the use of questions. Suggestions include:

1 Can you find a line with a word you could add an action to?
2 Can you find a line with more than two words beginning with the same letter?
3 Can you find two rhyming words, at the end of lines, which only have one letter that is different?
4 If the first line was changed to:
  It's distressing! It's upsetting! Shouldn't happen in your <u>house</u>
  how would you alter the second line?
5 Which verse is your favourite and why?

The list can easily be adapted and extended so that it can be used in conjunction with other poems. You can develop your own questions for other poems. Use questions that are literal, inferential and evaluative to broaden the cognitive demands placed on the children.

The five questions given here represent an early form of text deconstruction and, though form is not of greater importance than content, it is helpful for younger pupils to comprehend aspects of poetic organisation.

National Literacy Strategy Links

Year 2 Term 1 T.7: to learn, re-read and recite favourite poems… to comment on aspects such as word combinations, sound patterns (such as rhymes, rhythms, alliterative patterns) and forms of presentation.

Dis/continuities

Andrew Taylor

I began with a tiger and ended with a tail
The stripes in the middle withered and went stale.

I began with a leopard and ended with a spot
Something among trees diminished to a dot.

I began with a camel and ended with a hump
footprints meandering here to the Black Stump.

I began with a wolf and ended with a howl
so tiny it evaded even the owl.

I began with a whale and ended with a minnow
the whale's song echoing its sorrow.

I began with a forest and ended with a tree
in a paddock of sheep, lean and lonely.

I began with a sheep and ended with a fleece
and stolen knitwear softly pursued by police.

I began with an eagle and ended with a fall
from an altitude where everything looked small.

I began with the rabbit that the eagle saw,
Between grass and burrow came the sky's claw.

I began with a poem and ended with a list.
Wherever it takes you, follow each twist.

Dis/continuities (Andrew Taylor)

Andrew Taylor's wonderful poem includes much that is complex. Yet, when used with children at the top end of KS1, this is not off-putting as the playful, consistent structure is so appealing. One aspect of interest when reading a poem like this with children is the elusiveness of its meaning. Even if the meaning is not fully grasped, most pupils will not fail to note the poet's delight in the use and combination of words (it is a good lesson to learn that many of the most interesting things in life are not easily understood or fathomed!). After reading and discussing the poem, try these two activities.

Activity one: Materials and end – products poems

Loosely based on the format of Taylor's poem, the title I use for this activity in workshops is 'What will they become?' Start by writing the following half-finished lines on the board:

> *It began with some paper and ended with...*
> *It began with some cloth and ended with...*
> *It began with some bricks and ended with...*

Then ask the pupils to suggest what the paper could become. (The most frequent answer is 'a book'.) Depending upon the ability of the group you could either ask the pupils to complete further half-finished lines or ask them, in groups of three or four, to write further lines entirely by themselves. Other half-finished lines you could use are:

> *It began with a teabag and ended with...*
> *It began with a match and ended with...*

Activity two: It started with...

More closely related to Taylor's original poem, this activity can be used to focus on collective nouns. The pupils, once again, are shown several half-finished lines.

> *It started with a flock and ended with a...*
> *It started with a herd and ended with a...*
> *It started with a pack and ended with a...*

Then ask the children: 'What animals do you find in flocks?' (If answers are not forthcoming, resort to making an appropriate animal noise!) When you have reached an appropriate answer, such as sheep, ask the pupils: 'If all the flock but one got lost, what would we be left with?' The line can then be completed with the word 'sheep'. Continue the process until you have developed a poem that may become part of a 'Class Writing Display'.

National Literacy Strategy Links

Year 2 Term 1 T.12: to use simple poetry structures and to substitute own ideas, write new lines.

29

KS1 poem

My Life! By Chris Packet

I used to be useful
though nobody noticed.

I kept my crisps crunchy,
kept water out,
kept myself to myself
on the shelf
with my friends
in a neat line.

One day it was bound to happen –
torn apart, my insides eaten,
My thin body ready for the bin.

But I was tossed down,
run down,

swallowed by a swallow
(and that was the end of it!)
gulped down by a greyhound
(and that was the end of it too!)
blown on the breeze
into trees,
then the sea
where a fish ate me
(And guess what, that's the end!).

My Life! By Chris Packet

The obvious pun of the title (Chris Packet = Crisp Packet!) gives the game away – this poem is an example of personification. When we personify an inanimate object we attach human characteristics to it. With KS1 children I call these 'Bringing things to life' poems!

First, invite the pupils to choose a non-living object in the classroom, such as a book. Then write the following line openings and endings on the board.

> **I am (object chosen) a book**
> *I like…*
> *I don't like…*
> *I'm happy when…*
> *I'm sad when…*
> *I'm frightened of…*
> *…makes me angry*
> *… makes me glad*

Then ask the pupils to imagine that they are the chosen object, e.g. a book, and can speak. Ask the following question (naming the chosen object):

> *What do you like, book?*

The children then have to reply appropriately:

> *I like being read*

Write the answer on the board and add the word 'because' to the end of the sentence.

> *I like being read because…*

Ask the pupils to say why they like being read. For example,

> *I like being read because it's boring being left on the shelf*

Once this process has been modelled, and collectively written on the board, each pupil can choose a different object and write a personification poem by completing a pre-prepared set of line openings and endings, as above.

The activity can be differentiated by taking away the scaffold of line openings/ endings, thereby allowing more able pupils to produce lines entirely of their own making.

National Literacy Strategy Links

Year 2 Term 1 T.12: to use simple poetry structures and to substitute own ideas, write new lines.

If I was the Air

KS1 poem

If I was the air
I would blow through the trees,
Shake up the branches,
Rattle the leaves,
Hardly be noticed
Or come in a rush,
Tear off the roof tiles,
Create quite a fuss,
Make your hair crazy,
Blow off your hat,
Howl all around you,
How about that?

But if you were clever,
You'd even the score,
You'd take in a breath
And you'd finish the war,
I'd not have a choice,
I'd fly right up your nose,
I guess if I'm honest
It just goes to show,
I'd rather be me
Than a gale or a breeze,
I'd rather be me than the wind in the trees,
I'd rather be me
Than a typhoon or draught,
I may be just seven
But Hey! I'm not daft!!!

If I was the Air

If I was the Air is a type of list poem: basically it is an account of all the things a person would do if they became 'the air'. List poems are ideal models for pupils' own writing. They can also be used to develop speculative thinking. In order to do this, begin by reading the poem and asking the children: 'What if you were (example chosen) a raindrop, what would you do?'

This question is best asked of the whole class, and can form the basis of a brainstorming session. Write all the answers on the board, in the order that they are offered. (To maximise ideas, it may be useful to pair pupils with a 'Talk Buddy' and ask them to discuss their ideas together before sharing them with the whole class.)

Once a list of ideas has been generated, then the more complex task of ordering them into the lines of a poem is undertaken. Explain that there are many ways of doing this, and explore one or a combination of methods. Successful grouping strategies to use with Year 2 pupils include:

- Similar ideas
- Ideas that are funny!
- Ideas that would have a positive effect (ideas that would help people or things)
- Ideas that would have a negative effect (ideas that would harm people or things)
- Ideas that begin with the same letter of the alphabet
- Ideas that rhyme

The above list is only a starting point. The challenge of carefully grouping ideas when crafting a poem is worth exploring with pupils on a range of occasions – it is a fundamental part of writing an effective poem, regardless of whether this is for an audience of children or adults.

National Literacy Strategy Links

Year 2 Term 2 T.15: to use structures from poems as a basis for writing, by extending or substituting elements, inventing own lines, verses… to write own poems from initial jottings and words.

Teachers' notes

Tree
(A growing poem)

Seed
it grows
it gets bigger
fighting for the light
more now than a sapling
it's the tallest in the forest
it's the most beautiful fully grown tree.

Tree (A growing poem)

Tree is an example of a growing or expanding poem. It combines literacy with numeracy as each line is one word longer than the last. It is a type of list poem like *If I was the Air* (page 32), but the rigid numerical nature of its construction makes it somewhat more difficult to write.

Once the poem opposite has been read with the pupils, discuss the expanding nature of each line. Then, choose an alternative subject: this could be an object in the classroom or something related to work being undertaken in a different area of the curriculum, such as science or geography.

Pupils then play 'Tell me about it!' – a brainstorming game in which everything that is known about the object or subject is discussed and written on the board (by you or by each pupil as they suggest an idea). When information about the subject has been exhausted, the ideas are arranged/manipulated and rewritten beside the appropriate number on an 'Expanding poem line drafting grid'. This is simply a list of numbers beside which appropriate lines can be written. For example:

Expanding poem line drafting grid

1
2
3
4
5
6
7
8

A completed 'Expanding poem line drafting grid'

1   Water
2   It's wet
3   We drink it
4   Fish live in it
5   You can sail on it
6   When it freezes it becomes ice
7   Our bodies are mainly made of water
8   Water falls down on the earth as rain

Once you have modelled an example together, the children can choose a different subject/theme and, in groups of three or four, write their own expanding poem. An alternative is to write contracting poems – these begin with a ten-word line, and each subsequent line is one word shorter.

National Literacy Strategy Links

Year 2 Term 2 T.15: to use structures from poems as a basis for writing, by extending or substituting elements, inventing own lines, verses… to write own poems from initial jottings and words.

35

My Teacher is an Alien

My teacher is an alien,
My teacher is a bug,
It's awful when she's friendly,
I yell 'Don't give me a hug,
Don't try to embrace me with your sucker-covered arms,
Do not try and win me round with other-planet charms,
Don't stare when I'm naughty with your huge expanding
   eyes,
Do not try and frighten me with shrill galactic cries!'

Then Miss took us down the park and flew into a tree,
Throwing several conkers down, including one for me,
I must say that I've warmed to her,
She isn't all that bad,
Perhaps next week I'll introduce my teacher to my dad!

KS1 poem

My Teacher is an Alien

One of the great joys of writing poetry is the careful manipulation of words and ideas to generate a humorous response from the reader. 'Think weird' approaches help pupils to produce ideas that are humorous.

My Teacher is an Alien is an example of a 'think weird' poem. To help pupils to produce such poems you will find it helpful to initiate a planning/thinking stage prior to writing. In order to structure the planning stage in a meaningful way, each pupil should first choose a subject. This must be a physical thing, such as a *book*, rather than a theme, such as *holidays*. They then answer the following seven questions, which aim to stimulate tangential, surreal thought.

1   What might it do that would surprise you?
2   What else could it be made of?
3   If it could do anything at all, what would it choose to do?
4   What would make it laugh?
5   Where would it like to go?
6   If it could speak, what would it say?
7   If there was one thing it could change about itself, what would it be?

The answers to these questions form the basis of the poem (this works best when modelled as a shared writing experience prior to individual/small group writing). A major benefit of this approach is that it ensures that ideas are the 'driving force' behind the poem – with pupils in KS 1 this is worth stressing, as a focus on rhyme can lead to a loss of meaning. The pupils' need to rhyme can become the 'driving force' of the poem, rather than maintenance of the theme/ sense of the piece.

Subjects/titles that have proved consistently successful in workshops include:

• The X that was made of X, e.g. The car that was made of jelly
• The X that could X, e.g. The piano that could talk
• The X that went to X, e.g. The doll that went to the moon

National Literacy Strategy Links

Year 2 Term 3 T.8: to discuss meanings of words and phrases that create humour, and sound effects in poetry, e.g. nonsense poems, tongue-twisters, riddles, and to classify poems into simple types.

The Bibble Bumbi

I dreamt about my Bibble Bumbi,
All day long, about my Bumbi,
Bumbi beautiful and blarey
Bumbi brighter than canary,
Bumbi bellowing 'BURUPER!'
Bumbi playing Bumbi-snooker
Oh Bumbi, who sang fine Brumbazis,
Who played the grand Efozifazi,
Bumbi brughter than the lot
Whose favourite words were 'What' and 'What',
Bumbi, who once danced on ice,
Is now in Bumbi-Paradise,
I miss my Bumbi more and more
My nose is wet, my eyes are sore
Dear Bumbi who was Bibble clever
Has gone for Bibble Bumbi ever!

The Bibble Bumbi

There is a long tradition of writing nonsense poems for children – the most famous exponents of the form are undoubtedly Edward Lear and Lewis Carroll. If you wish to use a broader range of examples than the one opposite, the relevant websites on page 50 will prove invaluable.

Nonsense poems can be pure 'language play', with a focus on sound and rhythm rather than meaning. For the reluctant writer, the advantage of writing nonsense poems is that they can invent words, thereby making the process non-threatening.

After reading *The Bibble Bumbi*, explain to the children that they are going to invent a creature and write a nonsense poem about it, inventing as many words as they want. The pupils then close their eyes while you ask careful questions, encouraging them to visualise their creature prior to starting to write. The following series of multi-sensory questions may be helpful:

1   Picture your creature in your head. What are you going to call it?
2   What does its head look like?
3   What does its body look like?
4   Now touch it. What does it feel like?
5   Is there anything unusual about it?
6   How does it move around?
7   What does it like to do?
8   What doesn't it like to do?

At this point, tell the children to open their eyes and discuss their creature with a partner before they start writing their nonsense poem. (The poems can be rhyme or free verse.)

For struggling pupils, using a writing scaffold may help. For example:

> *It's called…*
> *It sounds like…*
> *It feels like…*
> *It can…*
> *It can also…*
> *The strangest thing about it is…*
> …………………………………
> …………………………………
> …………………………………

When producing a piece of writing structured like the example above, pupils should be encouraged to write their own lines, without sentence starters, at the end of the scaffold. This helps to develop their self-confidence, particularly if you gradually increase the number of lines they write independently.

National Literacy Strategy Links

Year 2 Term 3 T.8: to discuss meanings of words and phrases that create humour, and sound effects in poetry, e.g. nonsense poems, tongue-twisters, riddles, and to classify poems into simple types.

KS1 poem

Altered Nursery Rhymes

The True Tale of Humpty Dumpty

Humpty Dumpty sat on a wall,
Humpty Dumpty had a great fall,
All the King's horses and all the King's men
Have never been as shocked as then,
For Humpty bounced into the sky,
You should have seen old Humpty fly,
Through the rain and through the snow,
You should have seen old Humpty go,
He bounced along just like a ball
I'm really pleased he had his fall!

Baa Baa Green Sheep!

Baa Baa Green Sheep,
You look very weird,
Yes sir, yes sir
The others disappeared.
One in a spacecraft,
A shiny U.F.O,
There's only me left sir
And I've no place to go.

KS1 poem

Twinkle Twinkle Row of Teeth

Twinkle, twinkle, row of teeth,
Dazzling beyond belief,
Brushed on mornings, brushed at night,
These molars are a splendid sight,
The brightest thing I've looked upon,
I always put sunglasses on!

KS1 *poem*

Altered Nursery Rhymes

Altering nursery rhymes is a stimulating, fun writing task that always appeals to pupils. To adapt something that already exists is infinitely less complex than producing one's own poem from scratch. There is also a wealth of supportive published material that can be used as a stimulus for pupils, e.g. Roald Dahl's *Revolting Rhymes* (Jonathon Cape Ltd., 1982) and Michael Rosen's *Hairy Tales and Nursery Crimes* (Collins, 1987).

The two most popular ways of adapting a nursery rhyme are:

1   to alter the situation,
2   to alter the character trait.

Begin by reading a nursery rhyme in its original form, and follow this by reading an altered version of it. Then discuss the differences – *discussion/talk is a tremendously important part of the writing process.* Now read the nursery rhyme that the children will be adapting. Write pupils' suggestions for how to change it on the board. In pairs, the pupils can then write their own altered version.

If it is difficult for the children to generate ideas in this open-ended way, then the following usually work as a precursor to writing:

1   Read *Little Bo Peep*. Ask the children 'What else could she lose?' then 'What would she do next?'.
2   Read *Jack and Jill*. Ask the children 'Where else could they be going?' then 'Why?'.
3   Read *There was an old woman who lived in a shoe*. Ask the children 'What else could she live in?' then 'Why would she live there?'.

Any collection of nursery rhymes will suffice as a starting point, but those that are well illustrated and in a large format are usually more appealing and memorable.

National Literacy Strategy Links

Year 2 Term 3 T.11: to use humorous verse as a structure for children to write their own by adaptation, mimicry or substitution; to invent own riddles, language puzzles, jokes, nonsense sentences etc., derived from reading; write tongue-twisters or alliterative sentences; select words with care.

A Riddle

People talk of turning me over,
Sometimes I'm fastened high above you,
At other times I rush along the ground,
I can ride the wind,
There are many of me in the book you're reading.
What am I?

Answer: A leaf
People talk of turning over a new leaf.
Leaves can be fastened to trees.
In Autumn leaves rush along the ground.
Leaves can ride the wind and be blown around.
Each page in a book is called a 'leaf'.

A Riddle

Inventing riddles is not as simple a process as it might appear. In order to write a riddle, pupils need to understand that it provides clues to what its object is, *but does not name it*. Often, riddles are written in the first person, so they can be taught after work on personification (See *My Life! By Chris Packet*, page 30).

As with several of the other forms discussed in this book, using a scaffold when producing a riddle can be a useful first step towards a child's independent writing. The following is an example of a structural scaffold for a riddle:

I have...
I also have...
I can...
I can also...
....
What am I?

You can easily adapt this structure to include key words that the children may be learning.

Once this simple form of riddle has been learned, motivate pupils by asking them to produce difficult riddles for their classmates to solve. 'Riddle challenges' can then be played!

This poetic form is ideally suited to cross-curricular application. You can provide key words from other areas of the curriculum for 'riddling'. This is a useful way of assessing pupils' understanding of subject-specific words – it is impossible to produce a riddle for a word that has not been understood!

National Literacy Strategy Links

Year 2 Term 3 T.11: to use humorous verse as a structure for children to write their own by adaptation, mimicry or substitution; to invent own riddles, language puzzles, jokes, nonsense sentences etc., derived from reading; write tongue-twisters or alliterative sentences; select words with care.

KS1 poem

The Day My Head Fell Off

I wheezed, I huffed, my teeth all chattered,
My perfect health was left in tatters,
My eyes were sore, my nose was red,
I'd had hot lemon, lain in bed
…But nothing could prepare me for
the day my head fell on the floor!

We've all had colds, we hate the flu,
But this disease was something new,
It started with a stuffed up nose,
I'd given it a thousand blows,
And then, with an almighty cough,
The head I'm fond of fell right off!

It rolled about, came to a halt,
My brother yelled, 'It's not my fault'!
At first, with no clue what to do,
I looked up from my worm's eye view
Then, in a flash, I made a plan
That centred round a boy called Dan.

He's cruel, he's wicked, thinks he's great,
You've guessed that Dan is not my mate,
He likes to bully, sneak attack,
But now, I knew, I'd pay him back,
I'd shock him with a trick alright,
I'd give the lad a GIANT FRIGHT!

I picked my head up, placed it on
The neck where it had just come from,
It sometimes wobbled, sometimes shook,
But no-one gave a second look,
As people think that heads stay on,
Yet you and I know… they're all wrong!

And soon, stood in the school playground
I had my first good look around
And there he was, the brute, the cad,
The human who just sums up 'bad',
Shouting 'What you looking at?'
Brandishing a cricket bat!

And then I held my head up high,
Gripping it on either side,
Up there like a football cup,
It made the bully, Dan, shut up.
And then he whimpered, 'Help! Oh No!
Is that the time? I have to go!'

And off he ran and people cheered,
As we all watched him disappear,
And no-one laughed, and no-one scoffed,
I'm really pleased my head fell off!

The Day My Head Fell Off

The Day My Head Fell Off is an example of humorous story telling in verse. If you wish to provide further examples of this type of poetry then Colin McNaughton's collection, *There's an awful lot of weirdos in our neighbourhood: a book of rather silly verse and pictures* (Walker, 1989), contains numerous, popular examples.

An interesting activity to undertake after reading such a poem is 'genre modification'. In the classroom, this is more easily understood as 'turn a story into a poem'. This is most successful when using simple stories, such as fairy tales or familiar reading books, as a starting point. Read the story with the children who are then, usually in pairs, challenged to 'turn it into a poem'. It may be beneficial to model this process with the whole class as a shared writing exercise, prior to the children working in pairs.

A more open-ended activity is 'Writing to a title'. Provide pupils with a humorous title (or ask them to suggest ideas). Pupils can then be challenged to write a funny poem to fit it. Motivate the children by turning this into a competition and encouraging individuals to perform their written composition. The class can vote for their favourite poem and a suitable prize can be offered.

Titles that have proved successful in workshop sessions include:

- My teacher is an Alien
- The day I found I could fly
- My best friend, the dinosaur
- The world's worst shopping trip
- The school trip that went wrong!

It is essential to talk through these ideas adequately before pupils begin writing their poems. Time invested in discussion undoubtedly impacts on the quality of the finished poems.

National Literacy Strategy Links

Year 2 Term 3 T.11: to use humorous verse as a structure for children to write their own by adaptation, mimicry or substitution; to invent own riddles, language puzzles, jokes, nonsense sentences etc., derived from reading; write tongue-twisters or alliterative sentences; select words with care.

Teachers' notes

Skip Along

Skip along, skip along, one, two, three,
Open my eyes and what do I see?

Skip along, skip along, three, four, five,
A big bee buzzing around a bee hive,

Skip along, skip along, four, five, six,
Insects camouflaged to look like sticks,

Skip along, skip along, seven, eight, nine,
A slow snake winding round a vine,

Skip along, skip along, …only ten,
I guess it's time to start again.

Skip Along

Poems based on numbers are relatively simple to adapt. For example, pupils can:

1 Write alternative even lines. Instead of:

Skip along, skip along, one, two, three,
Open my eyes and what do I see?

Pupils could write something like:

Skip along, skip along, one, two, three,
If I wasn't a human what could I be?*

2 Write extensions:

Skip along, skip along, eleven, twelve, thirteen,
Can you guess what I have seen?

3 Write a poem using an alternative counting system. For example, in tens:

Skip along, skip along, ten, twenty, thirty,
Fell down in the mud and got really dirty.

Alternatively, you may wish to encourage the children to play with syllables and words so that their poem has a hidden numerical structure rather than the obvious numerical basis of the example provided.

To produce such a poem, first remind the children that syllables are parts of words, e.g. water has two parts, wa–ter. These can be clapped to reinforce the idea. Pupils can then be invited to make up sentences about a given subject, and to count the syllables. They are then asked to change the sentences (by adding, subtracting or changing words) so that each sentence has a fixed number of syllables – ten works well! Each of these ten-syllable sentences then becomes a line of the poem.

As with other activities in this book, this one is best modelled in a shared writing session prior to handing over responsibility for writing to smaller groups of pupils and, ultimately, individual writers.

National Literacy Strategy Links

Year 2 Term 3 T.11: to use humorous verse as a structure for children to write their own by adaptation, mimicry or substitution; to invent own riddles, language puzzles, jokes, nonsense sentences etc., derived from reading; write tongue-twisters or alliterative sentences; select words with care.

Teachers' notes

*You may wish to provide this alternative second line as a starting point for a new poem.

Useful websites

Nonsense Poems

http://f2.org/humour/language/nonsense.html
A useful, no-frills site with a range of nonsense poems by various authors. The variety is impressive and covers an assortment of styles.

http://edwardlear.tripod.com
The Edward Lear home page is slow to load but worth the wait. All of Lear's illustrated limericks (and more) are available in a few clicks. As they come in 'bite-size' portions, they are readily assimilated by pupils.

http://www.durrant.demon.co.uk/alice
This is a site that demonstrates how Lewis Carroll parodied familiar rhymes of the period when writing *Alice in Wonderland.* The originals are published alongside the parodies, which may be useful when planning lessons.

http://www.waxdog.com/jabberwocky/welcome.html
Here you will find all you ever wanted to know about the poem *Jabberwocky.* The site even includes definitions of all the nonsense words. Pupils will find it fascinating and hopefully stimulating.

Altered Nursery Rhymes

http://www.collingsm.freeserve.co.uk
A very comprehensive range of nursery rhymes categorised alphabetically and by subject.

Snaith Primary School Website
http://home.freeuk.net/elloughton13
For nursery rhymes (and other curricular components) try this brilliant site which has been prepared with children in mind. Suffice to say that the numerous links are well chosen and obviously child friendly.

Nursery Rhymes
www.indiaparenting.com/rhymes/english/er073.shtml
This site is meticulously prepared and has an extensive choice of nursery rhymes.

Nursery rhymes and their origins
www.geocities.com/Heartland/Valley/2161/nursery.html
A brief, but fascinating, introduction to the origin of nursery rhymes. This will whet the appetite.

Riddles

Just riddles and more
www.justriddlesandmore.com

There are lots of riddles for 'kids'. In addition there is a range of other options including Trivia, Teasers, Interactive word games and quizzes.

AZKidsNet
www.azkidsnet.com/riddles.htm
This site is easy to navigate and has a good range of material.

Preschool Fingerplays, Action poems, Nursery rhymes and songs

www.preschoolrainbow.org/preschool-rhymes.html
This site is easy to use and has an extensive range of fingerplay and action poems. Access them by clicking on either rhymes and songs or fingerplays on the navigator bar – then make your choice! The links are extensive.

University of South Carolina
www.libsci.sc.edu/miller/Transportation.htm
Two action poems relating to transport are included in this lesson plan.

ISMLC Poetry for Children
http://falcon.jmu.edu/~ramseyil/poechild.htm
This is a good site with loads of child friendly links to poetry sites.
The 'Fingerplays Index page' can be accessed from this site.

http://falcon.jmu.edu/~ramseyil/fingerplayindex.htm
As its name implies this site has an extensive range of fingerplay poems.

Seasonal Poetry

Poems for teachers and poems for children – Nancy's Teachers Resources
www.geocities.com/Heartland/1133/2teach.html
This site was compiled by a dedicated teacher and includes an interesting range of seasonal poems. I particularly liked the snowmen section.

Poets Page
http://sunniebunniezz.com/poetry/poetpage.htm
A wealth of seasonal poetry (amongst others) for children is readily available on this site.

Themed Poetry

Theme Poetry
www.tooter4kids.com/classroom/theme_poetry.htm
There are 30 themes of poetry on this easy to use and beautifully prepared site. Children will love it.

Robert Louis Stevenson
www.bartleby.com/188/index1.html

In this wonderful anthology, 'A Child's Garden of Verses and Underwoods', there is much to choose. My personal favourite is 'The Child Alone' collection.

Tooter4Kids
www.tooter4kids.com/frogs/poetry.htm
Here we have a frog theme collection specifically for children – a delightful website!!!

Pitara.com – Kids Network
www.pitara.com
This site includes an extensive and excellent poetry section which has a theme of animal poetry running throughout. The poems give an insight into Indian culture.

Alphabet Poems

Kids Corner
www.neighbourhood.com.au/AlphabetPoem.htm
Here is a good example of an alphabet poem dating from the 17th C. Follow this up by clicking on 'The Parson's Cat'.

Funny poets.com
www.funnypoets.com/theatozoflife.htm
Please note that some categories on this site are adult orientated but the alphabet poem is worth persuing as is the altered nursery rhyme 'Big Mary'. (Access this from Nursery Rhymes and fictional characters.)

Can Teach
www.canteach.ca/elementary/songspoems36.html
This Canadian site provides a range of alphabet poems which will be fun in a primary class. Click on 'Songs and Poems' for themed and seasonal poetry. Verdict – brilliant.

Personification

Poetry as we see it – Thinkquest
http://library.thinkquest.org/J0112392/index.html
As an introduction to personification this is excellent. There are examples and links to classic personification poems.

Shape/Concrete Poetry

Shape Poetry at Learn.co.uk
www.learn.co.uk
Enter this site, click on English Literature – Poetry under KS3 to reveal some clear examples of shape poetry.

Concrete Poem
www.risd.org/sitweb/Lessons/Poetry%20WP/Concrete%Poems.doc

Here you will find a suitable introduction for children. If you have difficulty in accessing the site go to www.risd.org, curriculum, lessons, then Concrete Poems.doc – its worth the effort!

Court's Concrete Creations
http://oregonstate.edu/~smithc/poems
Go here for more excellent examples